The Ten Commandments of Credit

BY

John J. Hudock

The Ten Commandments of Credit.

First Printing, June 2013

Published by DebtPros21.

DebtPros21 is dedicated to educating consumers about the credit industry. For more information please visit our website at *www.debtpros21.com*, or write to us at:

DebtPros21
401 Cooper St.
Taylor, PA 18517

Author: John J. Hudock
Chief Editor: Kenn Anderson, Jr.
Layout and Design: Kenn Anderson, Jr.

ISBN13: 978-0-9895831-4-5

Disclaimer

Please realize what am giving you to consider is my own opinion. It has been compiled from comparing thousands of credit reports, reviewing articles in publications, accessing web sites from the FTC, FICO and the credit repositories and then filtering the questionable data and recording the consistent.

All of the "factoring" (actual score reductions) is considered proprietary with FICO and the credit repositories. They concern themselves that with this information you would be able to manipulate your credit score.

I do not feel this is any misuse of information—it is your credit score—you should practice sound credit conduct to improve your credit score. Unfortunately, unless you are aware of the methods of scoring you can not know what actions affect your specific score and how to act accordingly.

John J. Hudock

Contents

Forward - The Evolution of Credit 7

1.) Pay your bills on time. NEVER more than 30 days late. 11

2.) Budget your income.......... 13

3.) Use credit cards to your advantage.......... 15

4.) Protect your identity.......... 17

5.) View your credit report at least once per year. 19

6.) Understand GOOD and BAD credit. 21

7.) Don't pay late accounts without an agreement. 23

8.) Understand what a credit score is. 25

9.) Avoid Credit Score Deductions.......... 31

10.) Know your credit rights. 33

Forward - The Evolution of Credit.

One of the first recorded references to credit was in 1950 BC. The King of Eshnunna (east bank of the Tigris) decreed a limit on the amount of interest (20%), and allowed borrowers grain and goods for loans made in silver.

In Babylon 1763 BC, King of Babylon (Code of Hammurabi) also limited interest to 20%. Borrowers could also sell their wife, son or daughter into slavery to settle debts. He added protection for those sold into indenture to three years, in the fourth year they would be given their freedom.

Modern banking was developed in northern Italy in 1215. The first bankers were money changers sitting on small benches in the market place. The word 'bank' is derived from the Italian word for 'bench', 'ban co'.

In 1780, George Washington's Yorktown campaign was financed with a loan arranged by Robert Morris, who was later imprisoned for land-speculation debts.

The first U.S. bankruptcy law was adopted in 1800 in response to losses suffered by land speculators; voluntary bankruptcy filings were not allowed until 1841.

In 1803, Members of the Mutual Communication Society of London shared information on credit risks. This was in London, England. The first United States credit bureau began in 1869 in Brooklyn, New York.

Fair Isaac Company (FICO)—Founded in 1956 by Bill Fair & Earl Isaac, FICO developed a scoring system using a specific combination of item scoring & factoring which can predict an individuals potential credit default risk - MATHEMATICALLY. These scores are reported through each of the credit bureaus, using different but similar scoring models. Mr. Isaac died in 1996.

Remember, the credit scoring system does not weigh sufficient information about your current financial situation. It cannot consider substantial increases in income and continues to reflect past adverse actions on your credit report.

FICO is placing too much emphasis on your past history which may, or may not, be a true representation of your current ability to repay any loan.

The Fair Credit Reporting Act (FCRA) states that your credit report is to reflect your credit worthiness to determine your ability to repay your loan. I doubt factors that are 7 to 10 years old could have the negative effect they are allowing to influence your score and are in any way relative to today's actual credit habits. Further, *there is no mandate* in the FCRA ,that negative credit information should remain on your report for 7 years. Your creditor can remove it at any time.

The Credit Bureaus use "Adverse Action Codes" to explain your deductions. One of the 38 deductions is Code# 97 (Lack of recent auto loan information). Interpreted, this means that if you do not have an auto loan there is a deduction in your score. There are now 38 codes but they are numbered up to 99 – they will add more.

The Credit Reporting Agencies (CRAs) are releasing new scoring models:

Experian............... **Advanced Risk Score**
Equifax................. **Pinnacle**
TransUnion.......... **Precision**

The Ten Commandments of Credit

1.) Pay your bills on time. NEVER more than 30 days late.

This should be the basis for good credit. Besides having the ability to repay a loan, your payment history is the next most important item. The trigger date for late payments is 30 days, then 60 days, 90 days etc. Each period is another category with a greater point deduction. It is very important to keep all credit accounts within the agreed payment period to establish credit.

If you are more than 30 days late, the account changes from an OPEN account to a DEROGATORY account. This is very serious because even if you pay your account current, or close the account, it will remain derogatory, lowering your credit score for up to seven years. You must arrive at a fair settlement with the creditor to report it as paid in full with NO DEROGATORY comments.

2.) Budget your income.

Setting up a budget is paramount in any successful personal financial plan – A budget is actually a plan for spending and saving your money. There are many benefits of having a budget.

Many individuals attempt to do this mentally but if your income ratio to expenses is close you must be able to see the reality of the numbers. Making and following a budget means you can have money for the things you want. When you are not tracking your expenses, cash always seems to disappear.

Income is the amount of money you make. **Expenses** are what you spend your money on. A balanced budget is when your income is at least as much as your expenses. The most important factor in budgeting is maintaining simple but accurate records. When starting your budget you will need to keep track of where your money comes from and where it goes. You should write down what you spend in a computer or notebook and try to keep receipts for what you spend.

Without a budget you do not know accurately where your money goes, and perhaps you can't afford things you would like to have. When you know where your money goes, you feel and actually have more control. It's easier to pay your bills on time, save money each month, and avoid money problems.

Start a checking account and get a debit card. That way, when you pay for purchases you will already have a record of them. This will reduce the individual expenses you must track to only the cash payments you make. A checking account will also provide a vehicle to establish an automatic method to make payments developing an excellent payment history.

Each month, compare your actual expenses to what you have in your budget. To make this work you must keep your spending within your plan, constantly looking for ways to reduce your expenses. You have more control over expenses than income.

It takes perseverance, especially in the beginning. It will take some time to set up a plan that works for you. You can make all the changes you need to make it work. The sooner you start the easier it will be.

3.) Use credit cards to your advantage.

There are many Credit Card considerations, The main consideration is to use your credit card as cash and pay the balance "IN FULL" every month.

Credit cards are good for two things:

1.) To increase your credit score
2.) For convenience.

You should **never** use credit cards for any long term credit – it is entirely too expensive. You increase the cost of anything you purchase using the credit card by over 20% unless you pay the balance in full each month. The higher the balances on you credit cards the more you lower your credit score and the more interest you pay on anything else.

It is ridiculous to pay the more than 20% extra using your card to purchase anything and then not paying the balance each month. Paying your balance each month could save you the 20% or more for other things you need or want.

You need to use each credit card once every six months. Credit card issuers are now canceling some credit card accounts if they are not used.

The current scoring system requires you to have at least 2 credit cards or revolving accounts – they claim the number is required to evaluate your payment habits. Actually you need three to four open trade-lines with each repository - credit cards are the most appropriate since they report to all three credit repositories. You should restrict the number and do not have more than 4 credit cards.

Never have any credit card without a "Grace Period." You need this time to control the expense. The grace period should be 20 to 25 days. TWO of the types of credit cards are **Unsecured** (requiring credit scores over 620) and **Secured** (requiring a deposit).

Normally, for a secured credit card, you need to deposit the amount of the credit card limit to get a credit card issued. Some programs will charge the amount of this to the credit card, then deposit this amount into a savings (low interest bearing) account. All secured cards charge an annual membership fee ($29.00 to $150.00) to your new credit card.

The current average interest rate is about 21%, but you should always have at least a 20 day to 25 day grace period. No interest is charged if balance is paid, in full, within 20 to 25 days from billing date. You could use the bank's money and pay each account in full when due and pay no interest.

Always check your monthly fee, and annual fee, and any other fee on your monthly statement. Read your agreement and keep your balance below 25% of your upper limit. Some credit cards will charge a late fee if they receive your payment on the day it is due. THIS IS ILLEGAL—contact the credit card issuer immediately and have the late fee removed.

4.) Protect your identity.

There is a difference between **Credit Theft** and **Identity Theft**. Credit theft (also known as credit fraud) is when someone makes purchases on accounts that are yours. They will take one or more of your credit card numbers and use them as their own. Even though credit theft can be difficult, it is no where near as hard to deal with as identity theft. Identity theft is when a criminal uses your personal information to open new accounts. In the case of identity theft, the criminal will obtain personal information about you and use that information to secure credit in your name for them to use. They will open these credit card accounts and take out loans in your name. It could range between anything, from auto loans, to home equity loans.

The six most important guards against identity theft are:

1.) You should guard your personal identifying information. Before divulging it, you should find out how it will be used and whether it will be transferred to third parties. They should find out whether they have the choice of "opting out" of having the information shared with third parties.

2.) You should insure that items containing personal information -- such as charge receipts, insurance forms and bank statements -- are disposed of safely.

3.) You should disclose your Social Security numbers only when absolutely necessary. You should ask to use alternate numbers as identifiers whenever possible, including on motor vehicle license

4.) You should periodically check your credit report.

5.) You should carry only the credit cards and identification you actually need. If you lose credit cards you should notify the creditors by phone and request that a "fraud alert" be placed in your file.

6.) You should pay attention to billing cycles. Bills that do not arrive on time may have been misdirected by identity thieves.

You can contact the national repositories with information relating to fraud at the following addresses and phone numbers:

Equifax Credit Information Services, Inc.
PO Box 105069
Atlanta, GA 30349
(800) 525-6285

Experian
PO Box 1017
Allen, TX 75013
(888) 397-3742

Trans Union
PO Box 6790
Fullerton, CA 92634
(800) 680-7289

5.) View your credit report at least once per year.

You must obtain and review a copy of your credit report from each of the three major credit reporting agencies at least once a year to make sure your information is accurate. The reports are free if you live in Colorado, Georgia, Massachusetts, Maryland, New Jersey, and Vermont. They will cost between $1.00 to $9.00 in the other states although they are free in all U.S. states if:

1.) You were denied credit, insurance or a job; or

2.) You are on welfare or unemployed and looking for work; or

3.) Your report is inaccurate due to fraud

The Fair and Accurate Credit Transactions Act (FACT) H.R. 2622, adopted in December 2003, provides all consumers a free copy of their credit report without the scores—one from each bureau, each year. For a free copy of your report, you can access the website at the address www.freecreditreport.com.

6.) Understand GOOD and BAD credit.

There isn't any constant or fixed deduction for any negative on your credit report. There is no specific reduction for any considered action —the deduction is relative to the entire credit report. This is called segmented scoring.

In calculating each tradeline deduction, we have assigned fixed numbers to develop relative actions. In the Mortgage Model, the Credit Bureaus designate an 850 as the highest score and the banks use a 720 as the highest score necessary for a preferred interest rate. This leaves 130 points that are not necessary.

The differences between a good credit score(*around 700*), a fair score (*around 640*), and a bad score (*below 600*) are where minor deficits in your credit profile can remain until resolved or deleted by time.

Consider the costs of a $20,000 car paid over 5 years:

CREDIT STATUS	RATE	COST OF BAD CREDIT
Good Score	5%	**$5,000.00**
Fair Score	7%	**$7,000.00**
Bad Score	9%	**$9,000.00**

Consider a $100,000 home paid over 30 years:

CREDIT STATUS	RATE	PAYMENT	COST OF BAD CREDIT
Good Score	3.5%	$ 602.00	**$ 105,000.00**
Fair Score	6%	$ 806.82	**$ 180,000.00**
Bad Score	9%	$1,030.67	**$ 270,000.00**

7.) Don't pay late accounts without an agreement.

I do not advocate that you do not pay any legitimate bills, but it is not to your advantage to pay off any late accounts over thirty days unless the creditor agrees to certain conditions. You should give your creditor two choices, either remove the tradeline from your credit report or mark the account closed with a zero balance with no additional comments. Unless you do this, even if the account is paid in full, it will remain as a derogatory account on your credit report for up to seven years.

It is quite difficult to legally restore your credit without somehow satisfying your outstanding debts. If it is a legal debt, you should always make an effort to pay it.

However, the act of paying off a debt can actually hurt your credit. Negative credit is allowed to stay on the credit report for a maximum of seven years, except for bankruptcy which may remain on the credit report for ten years. This seven year period, begins on Date of Last Activity (DLA), in other words, whenever the last action took place on the account.

By paying an outstanding, delinquent debt, you will change the account status to a "paid collection," "paid-was late," or "paid-was charged off" – which will still stand out as a very negative listing. Regardless of what the credit grantor states, it is not up to the repository as to what is on your credit report. The creditor reports what they want to the repository. They can enter or remove any tradeline and any information they determine is accurate, complete, and current. It is very important you receive in writing a satisfactory settlement before you pay off any derogatory account.

A payment could also change the DLA, so that it will start all over, increasing the time that this derogatory mark will stay on your credit report. It may be to your advantage to close all derogatory accounts and make arrangements to pay them, if the creditor will agree to a proper settlement agreement.

8.) Understand what a credit score is.

My first inclination was to suggest that you practice good credit habits and not to concern yourself with the credit score, but FICO and the three repositories will not let you do that. They have placed a very high importance on credit scores. Most scores are artificially low since they are based on inaccurate information. You must understand what factors make up your credit score and what you can do to increase this three digit number. For mortgages, the score ranges from a low of 350, to a high of 850. 720 and above is the preferred score for most lenders, giving you the lowest interest rates. 500 to 620 is sub-prime, with high interest rates. Anything below 500, generally, is too low for any type of credit. You probably need open lines of credit. The best and fastest method is to start with a secured credit card as they report to all three national credit bureaus.

When you have a spouse, I recommend getting one card in an individual name for each spouse. After 30 days, add your spouses name to each of the cards.

Your credit score is like a credit report reduced to a three digit number. Your FICO score, as it is generally called, was meant to be based on your credit history. If the credit information is accurate, the reflection is correct. Unfortunately, there are consistent errors in each credit report, causing at times, a dramatic lowering of the credit score.

Based on a scale model of 350 to 850, with 850 as the highest, there are one, two, or three scores – each score from one of the three national credit bureaus, using different but similar scoring models, all from FICO. Most lenders use the middle score. The current scoring models are in the process of being updated. They have determined more factors effect your creditworthiness, which I interpret as being incorrect. For example, if you do not have an auto loan or mortgage, there are deductions.

These three scores are what most lenders will look at when evaluating your credit for your loan applications. To understand this more clearly, see below how your score relationship affects costs based on an average par interest rate as of January 1, 2004.

Credit Score	Interest Rate	Cost/ 1000	Monthly Payment	Full 30 Yr Term
500 –559	9.62%	$8.50	$850.00	$306,000.00
560 –619	8.50%	$7.69	$769.00	$276,860.00
620 – 674	7.62%	$7.16	$718.00	$254,880.00
675 – 699	6.37%	$6.24	$624.00	$224,640.00
700 – 719	5.99%	$5.95	$595.00	$214,200.00
720 – 850	5.75%	$5.84	$584.00	$210,240.00

The above is based on the same amount of principal (**$100,000.00**) but the credit score causes the interest rate to go from 5.75% to 9.62%, increasing the monthly payments by $266.00 and the total paid to the bank by an additional $95,760.00.

Each of the national credit bureaus utilizes the FICO algorithm to provide credit scores. The bureaus each market their credit scores under a different name:

Fair Isaac Corporation continually upgrades its scoring models in order to provide the sharpest credit evaluation possible. The NextGen (Next Generation) credit score offers the latest innovations in credit risk analysis.

Credit Bureau	Credit Score Model	Next Generation Score Model
Experian	FICO or Ver. 2	FICO Advanced Risk Score
Equifax	BEACON®	Pinnacle(sm)
TransUnion	EMPIRICA®	Precision(sm)

In an attempt to justify the credit score FICO lists four of the following "Adverse Actions" for each repository on each credit report. It is intended to be an explanation to give to the consumer and illustrate the top four adverse conditions for the credit report.

Equifax/Beacon '96 lists the four major adverse actions using a five-digit number with the adverse code as the last two digits.

Transunion/Empirica lists the four major adverse actions using a three-digit number with the adverse code as the last two digits.

Experian/Fair Isaac (Ver. 2) lists the four major adverse actions using a 2 digit number with the adverse code as the only two digits.

All three repositories use the same code numbers for the same adverse action but do not list them in the same order on the credit report. Many times, there does not appear to be a relationship to the credit information and the codes.

There are currently 38 adverse actions in use. FICO is taking deductions from the credit for each of these that apply. Many actions are similar, using every tactic to reduce your credit score.

I feel that many of these considerations are inappropriate. For example, there is a deduction if you don't have an auto loan. If you haven't had any recent revolving account transactions, they lower your score. FICO should not have this indiscriminate power. They are totally biased and discriminate. I have seen this on thousands of credit scores. Being a low income person with a small credit history can have a significant negative effect on your score.

The following adverse notations are listed on each of the credit reports:

CODE #	ADVERSE ACTION DESCRIPTION
01	Amount owed on accounts too high
02	Delinquency on accounts too high
03	Too few bank revolving accounts
04	Too many revolving accounts
05	Too many accounts with balances
06	Consumer finance accounts
07	Account payment history too new to rate
08	Too many recent inquiries last 12 months
09	Too many accounts opened in last 12 months
10	Proportion of balances to credit limit too high
11	Amount owed on revolving accounts too high
12	Length of credit history too short
13	Time since delinquent is too recent
14	Lack of recent bank revolving history is short
16	Lack of recent revolving history is too short
17	No recent non-mortgage balance information
18	Number of accounts with delinquency
19	Too few accounts paid as agreed
20	Time since derogatory public record collection
21	Amount of past due on account
22	Serious delinquency, derogatory public records or collection
24	No recent revolving balances
28	Number of established accounts
30	Time since last account opening too short
31	Too few accounts with recent payment
32	Lack of recent installment loan information
33	Proportion of loan balances to loan amounts too high

CODE #	ADVERSE ACTION DESCRIPTION
34	Amount owed on delinquent accounts
35	Payments due on accounts
36	Length of time open accounts have been established
37	Number of consumer finance company accounts est./ relative to length of history
38	Serious delinquency and public records or collection filed
39	Serious delinquency
40	Delinquency public record or collection filed
47	Number of consumer finance co. inquiries
97	Lack of recent auto loan information
98	Length of time consumer co loans been established
99	Lack of recent consumer finance co acct. information

If you see any errors on your credit report, contact the creditor and the credit bureau. The three major bureaus phone numbers are:

Equifax	(**1-800-685-1111**)
Experian	(**1-888-397-3742**)
Trans Union	(**1-800-916-8800**)

If you do not receive cooperation from the repositories, call the FTC Federal Trade Commission at **1-877-382-4357** and issue a complaint.

9.) Avoid Credit Score Deductions.

You should maintain **at least 3 to 4 OPEN lines of credit** with each repository. An OPEN line is credit granted to you that you have paid, as agreed, from the day it was started. If you are more than 30 days late on any tradeline, it becomes a DEROGATORY account and will remain a derogatory account for up to SEVEN years, even if you pay all past due amounts or pay the account in full. You must have at least 2 OPEN lines of credit from creditors that report to the repositories, with each repository to have a credit score above 500. You must have at least 3 OPEN lines of credit to have a credit score above 600. There are five types of information used to calculate a credit score at any given point in time. Each type of information counts as a percentage of a total FICO score:

Payment history........................ 35%
Amounts owed.......................... 30%
Length of credit history.......... 15%
New credit................................ 10%
Types of credit in use.............. 10%

These are not fixed percentages for any deduction and they are based on the importance of the five categories for the general population. For particular individual groups, such as people with relatively short credit histories, the factoring of the categories will differ. Inquiries account for 10% of the total score and are part of the "new credit" category shown above. Their importance depends on the overall information in your credit report. For some people, a given factor may be more important than for someone else with a different credit history.

In addition, as the information in your credit report changes, so does the importance of any factor in determining your score. What's important is the mix of information, which varies from credit report to credit report and for any one person over time.

10.) Know your credit rights.

Federal Trade Commission – FTC (From the FTC Website). The FTC works for the consumer to prevent fraudulent, deceptive and unfair business practices in the marketplace and to provide information to help consumers spot, stop, and avoid them. To file a complaint or to get free information on consumer issues, visit www.ftc.gov or call toll-free, 1-877-FTC-HELP (1-877-382-4357); TTY: 1-866-653-4261. The FTC enters Internet, telemarketing, identity theft, and other fraud-related complaints into Consumer Sentinel, a secure, online database available to hundreds of civil and criminal law enforcement agencies in the U.S. and abroad.

Credit Card Information

Cardholder Protections—Federal law protects your use of credit cards.

Prompt Credit for Payment—An issuer must credit your account the day payment is received. The exceptions are if the payment is not made according to the creditor's requirements, or the delay in crediting your account won't result in a charge. To help avoid finance charges, follow the issuer's mailing instructions. Payments sent to the wrong address could delay crediting your account for up to five days. If you misplace your payment envelope, look for the payment address on your billing statement or call the issuer.

Refunds of Credit Balances—When you make a return or pay more than the total balance at present, you can keep the credit on your account or write your issuer for a refund - if it's more than a dollar. A refund must be issued within seven business days of receiving your request. If a credit stays on your account for more than six months, the issuer must make a good faith effort to send you a refund.

Errors on Your Bill—Issuers must follow rules for promptly correcting billing errors. You'll get a statement outlining these rules when you open an account and at least once a year. In fact, many issuers include a summary of these rights on your bills. If you find a mistake on your bill, you can dispute the charge and withhold payment on that amount while the charge is being investigated. The error might be a charge for the wrong amount, for something you didn't accept, or for an item that wasn't delivered as agreed. Of course, you still have to pay any part of the bill that's not in dispute, including finance and other charges.

If you decide to dispute a charge:

1.) Write to the creditor at the address indicated on your statement for "billing inquiries." Include your name, address, account number, and a description of the error.
2.) Send your letter soon. It must reach the creditor within 60 days after the first bill containing the error was mailed to you The creditor must acknowledge your complaint in writing within 30 days of receipt, unless the problem has been resolved. At the latest, the dispute must be resolved within two billing cycles, but not more than 90 days.

Unauthorized Charges—If your card is used without your permission, you can be held responsible for up to $50 per card. Provide reliable sources of the disputed information and inform them of the nature of the consumer's dispute." In some cases, if you report the loss before the card is used, you can't be held responsible for any unauthorized charges. If a thief uses your card before you report it missing, the most you'll owe for unauthorized charges is $50. To minimize your liability, report the loss as soon as possible. Some issuers have 24-hour toll-free telephone numbers to accept emergency information. It's a good idea to follow-up with a letter to the issuer - include your account number, the date you noticed your card missing, and the date you reported the loss.

Disputes about Merchandise or Services—You can dispute charges for unsatisfactory goods or services. To do so, you must have made the purchase in your home state or within 100 miles of your current billing address. The charge must be for more than $50. (These limitations don't apply if the seller also is the card issuer or if a special business relationship exists between the seller and the card issuer.) and, First make a good faith effort to resolve the dispute with the seller. No special procedures are required to do so.

If these conditions don't apply, you may want to consider filing an action in small claims court.

The Federal Trade Commission offers help and information. Questions about a particular issuer should be sent to the agency with jurisdiction.

National Banks
Comptroller of the Currency
Compliance Management
Mail Stop 7-5
Washington, DC 20219

State Member Banks of the Reserve System
Consumer and Community Affairs
Federal Reserve Board
20th & C Streets, NW
Washington, DC 20551

Federal Credit Unions
National Credit Union Administration
1776 G Street, NW
Washington, DC 20456

Non-Member Federally Insured Banks
Office of Consumer Programs
Federal Deposit Insurance Corporation
550 Seventeenth Street, NW
Washington, DC 20429

Federally Insured Savings and Loans, and Federally Chartered State Banks
Consumer Affairs Program
Office of Thrift Supervision
1700 G Street, NW
Washington, DC 20552

Other Credit Card Issuers (includes retail/gasoline companies)
Consumer Response Center
Federal Trade Commission
Washington, DC 20580

Office of The Inspector General—Consumer complaints and inquiries about possible law violations that are within the investigative purview of FTC enforcement staff should not be reported to the OIG, but rather to the FTC's Consumer Response Center (CRC).

Such possible law violations under the enforcement staff's authority include various deceptive acts or practices which could constitute a violation of the FTC Act, and activities which might violate one or more of the numerous other laws, rules, and regulations enforced by the FTC (for example, the often consumer-referenced: Fair Credit Reporting Act, Fair Debt Collection Practices Act, and the Telemarketing Sales Rule).

The CRC can be reached by telephone at **(202) FTC-HELP / (202) 382-4357**, or through the Internet at www.ftc.gov, where consumers can also access, complete and transmit to the CRC the FTC's Public

Complaint Form. All general inquiries about the FTC and its activities, other than those related to the OIG, should be directed to the agency's public telephone number: **(202) 326-2222**, which has menu options to connect callers to the CRC, as well as the agency's press and personnel offices, and to other frequently called FTC numbers.

Other Consumer Rights Literature

The Fair Credit Reporting Act (FCRA) is designed to help ensure that FCRAs furnish correct and complete information to businesses to use when evaluating your application.

The Equal Credit Opportunity Act (ECOA) prohibits credit discrimination on the basis of sex, race, marital status, religion, national origin, age, or receipt of public assistance

The Fair Credit Billing Act (FCBA) and **Electronic Fund Transfer Act (EFTA)** establish procedures for resolving mistakes on credit billing and electronic fund transfer account statements, including: charges or electronic fund transfers that you, or anyone you have authorized to use your account, have not made as well as charges or electronic fund transfers that are incorrectly identified or show the wrong amount or date; computational or similar errors; failure to reflect payments, credits, of electronic fund transfers properly; and not mailing or delivering credit billing statements to your current address.

The Fair Debt Collection Practices Act (FDCPA) applies to personal, family, and household debts.

Fair and Accurate Credit Transactions Act of 2003 (FACT) H.R. 2622 provides consumer protections against identity theft (that is, fraud committed using another person's identifying information).

FOR MORE INFORMATION, PLEASE CHECK OUT THESE OTHER PUBLICATIONS FROM DEBTPROS21.

Reading Your Credit Report

This book guides you through each individual trade line and tells you the significance of each piece of information as it applies to your credit worthiness, as well as the proper procedures for disputing errors on your credit information.

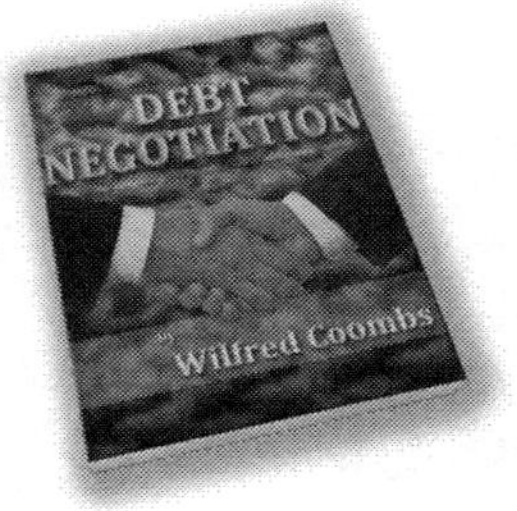

Debt Negotiation

If and when you decide to take on your credit problems yourself, here is a handy guide to the proper procedures you should follow to insure that you negotiate from strength and achieve the best possible results.

The Credit Industry

Learn about how to read your credit report, protect yourself from predatory lenders and debt collectors, as well as how to safeguard yourself from credit fraud and identity theft.

ISBN 978-0-9895831-4-5

9 780989 583145

Made in the USA
Monee, IL
04 November 2026

67382368R00022